About the Author: Raj C Vaidyamath - Entrepreneur ,Mentor and A Curious Mind !!!

Meet the passionate author, a lifelong learner, and a relentless explorer of knowledge who has dedicated their writing career to sharing valuable insights with readers around the world. With a profound curiosity about diverse subjects, including religion, traditions, and the transformative power of technology, particularly AI, the author brings a unique perspective to their work.

With a diverse range of books covering topics such as AI/ML technology, spirituality, finance, and the impact of technology on traditions, the author's writing offers comprehensive insights and practical knowledge. Through their carefully curated content and thought-provoking ideas, readers are empowered to navigate complex subjects and discover new perspectives.

Beyond their writing endeavors, the author brings a wealth of experience from working with renowned companies across different industries. Their professional journey has honed their skills in software engineering, team management, and ensuring exceptional customer satisfaction. However, it is their unwavering passion for knowledge, continuous learning, and personal growth that drives their true purpose.

Outside the realm of professional pursuits, the author's interests extend to the world of finance. As an avid Algo Trader, they delve into the intricacies of the stock market, investments, and financial education. With a commitment to analyzing market trends, employing algorithmic strategies, and embracing continuous learning, they strive to make informed decisions and maximize investment opportunities.

In summary, this accomplished author embodies the spirit of intellectual exploration and strives to inspire individuals through their writing. By delving into the intersections of technology, traditions, and personal growth, they aim to make a positive impact on the lives of readers, encouraging them to embrace continuous learning and discover new horizons of knowledge.

ABOUT THIS BOOK

"Vector Databases Unleashed: Navigating the Future of Data Analytics" offers a comprehensive exploration of vector databases through the lens of artificial intelligence, meticulously curated by the author to provide a blend of foundational knowledge, advanced technical insights, and forward-looking trends. This book delves into the heart of vector database technology, revealing its pivotal role in the evolution of data analytics and its indispensable use in AI applications. From the basic principles that underpin vector databases to the complex algorithms driving today's most advanced AI models, readers are guided through an in-depth examination of the mechanisms, applications, and transformative potential of these powerful database systems.

Each chapter is crafted with an Artificial Intelligence-curated perspective, ensuring that both the content and its presentation are aligned with the latest in AI-driven data analysis techniques. The book addresses not only the technical aspects of vector databases but also explores their societal impact, ethical considerations, and the future possibilities they herald for industries ranging from healthcare to finance. Through engaging case studies, practical examples, and a forward-thinking approach, "Vector Databases Unleashed" equips readers with the insights needed to navigate the rapidly evolving landscape of data analytics, making it an essential resource for professionals, researchers, and enthusiasts alike.

Authored with a keen eye on the future and a deep understanding of the transformative power of vector databases, this book stands as a testament to the synergy between human expertise and artificial intelligence in curating knowledge that is not only informative but also inspiring, paving the way for readers to harness the potential of vector databases in their own innovative applications.

INDEX

13	Advanced Techniques	Optimization Techniques	Optimizing VDB Performance	Strategies for optimizing vector database performance
14	Emerging Technologies	Quantum Computing	Quantum Computing & VDBs	The potential impact of quantum computing on VDBs
15	Emerging Technologies	Graph Databases	Integration with Graph DBs	Integrating vector and graph databases for advanced analytics
16	Case Studies	Industry Applications	Search in E-commerce	Enhancing e-commerce search with vector databases
17	Case Studies	Custom Solutions	Content Discovery	Content discovery in media and entertainment
18	Security and Privacy	Database Security	Security Best Practices	Best practices for securing vector databases
19	Security and Privacy	Data Privacy	Privacy in AI Applications	Ensuring data privacy in AI applications using VDBs
20	Industry Impacts	Healthcare	Personalized Medicine	Personalizing medicine with vector databases
21	Industry Impacts	Finance	Fraud Detection	Enhancing fraud detection with vector databases
22	Performance Tuning	Query Optimization	Query Optimization Techniques	Optimizing queries in vector databases for performance
23	Performance Tuning	Hardware Acceleration	Using Hardware Acceleration	Exploiting hardware acceleration for VDBs
24	Data Management	Data Ingestion	Efficient Data Ingestion	Strategies for efficient data ingestion into VDBs
25	Data Management	Data Governance	Data Governance in VDBs	Implementing data governance for vector databases
26	Development Practices	DevOps for VDBs	DevOps Practices	Integrating DevOps practices with vector database management

27	Development Practices	Testing and Validation	Testing VDB Applications	Testing and validating vector database applications
28	Future Directions	Edge Computing	Edge Computing and VDBs	Vector databases at the edge: Opportunities and challenges
29	Future Directions	Interoperability	Data Interoperability	Ensuring data interoperability among vector databases
30	Visualization Techniques	Visualization in VDBs	Visualizing Vector Data	Techniques for visualizing data in vector databases
31	Visualization Techniques	Interactive Analysis	Interactive Analysis Tools	Enabling interactive analysis with vector databases
32	Regulatory Compliance	Compliance Issues	Compliance Challenges in VDBs	Navigating regulatory compliance for vector databases
33	Regulatory Compliance	Auditing and Reporting	Auditing & Reporting Mechanisms	Implementing effective auditing and reporting in VDBs
34	Ethical Considerations	Ethical AI	AI Ethics in Vector Databases	Ethical considerations in the use of vector databases in AI
35	Ethical Considerations	Data Bias	Bias in Vector Data	Addressing bias in vector data and databases
36	International Perspectives	Global Adoption	Global Trends in VDB Adoption	Exploring the global adoption of vector databases
37	International Perspectives	Cross-Border Data Flow	Cross-Border Data Management	Managing cross-border data flows with vector databases
38	Career Development	Building Expertise	Skills Development	Developing skills for careers in vector databases
39	Career Development	Professional Growth	Career Pathways in VDBs	Exploring career pathways in vector databases
40	Future Outlook	Future Technologies	Next-Generation VDB Tech	Anticipating future technologies in vector databases

| 41 | Future Outlook | Impact on Society | Societal Impact of VDBs | Assessing the societal impact of vector databases |

Chapter 1: Vector Databases 101

Vector Data Defined

Overview of vector data and its importance

Vector Data Defined

Vector data is a fundamental concept in the realm of data analytics, particularly in the context of artificial intelligence and machine learning applications.

Simply put, vector data refers to data points represented in a multi-dimensional space.

These data points, also known as vectors, consist of numerical values organized in a specific order to create a geometric entity.

In the context of AI and ML, these vectors are utilized to represent complex datasets that may have numerous attributes or features.

Understanding vector data is crucial for grasping how vector databases function and how they optimize the storage and retrieval of information.

Vectors in vector databases play a key role in various AI and ML algorithms.

They provide a structured way to represent data that enables efficient processing and analysis.

By arranging data points in a multi-dimensional space, vectors help capture the inherent relationships and patterns within the data.

This structured representation is vital for tasks such as clustering, classification, and regression in AI/ML, where the goal is to identify patterns, make predictions, or group similar data points together.

Vector data's importance lies in its ability to enable complex mathematical operations on data, facilitating advanced analytics and decision-making processes.

In the context of database operations, vector data plays a crucial role in enabling efficient querying and indexing capabilities.

Vector databases leverage the mathematical properties of vector data to perform similarity searches, clustering, and other operations essential for AI/ML applications.

By utilizing vector representations of data, these databases can quickly identify similar data points or patterns, making them invaluable for tasks like recommendation systems, image recognition, and natural language processing.

In conclusion, grasping the fundamentals of vector data is essential for anyone working with AI/ML applications, as it forms the basis for efficient data representation, processing, and analysis in the field.

Chapter 2: Vector Databases 101

Architecture of VDBs

Exploring the architecture of vector databases

Exploring the architecture of vector databases reveals key elements that contribute to their suitability for AI applications and big data analytics.

At the core of this architecture is the efficient handling of vector data, which is fundamental to processing complex datasets prevalent in AI-driven scenarios.

One key architectural element is the indexing mechanisms employed by vector databases.

These mechanisms are specifically designed to optimize the retrieval of vector data, enabling rapid access and manipulation required for various machine learning algorithms.

By organizing data in a manner that facilitates efficient search and query operations, vector databases streamline the processing of large-scale datasets essential for AI applications.

In addition to indexing mechanisms, the data storage approach of vector databases plays a crucial role in their architectural design.

Vector databases are structured to store vector data in a manner that allows for quick retrieval and processing.

This involves techniques such as data partitioning, compression, and parallel processing to enhance the storage and access of vector data.

By implementing storage strategies that align with the characteristics of vector data, these databases can scale effectively and support the computational demands of AI algorithms.

Furthermore, the retrieval processes within vector databases are optimized to efficiently fetch vector data based on specific criteria, enabling AI applications to access and analyze data swiftly for tasks such as pattern recognition, clustering, and classification.

Another key aspect of the architecture of vector databases that makes them well-suited for AI applications is their support for specialized data structures and operations tailored to vector data.

These databases are designed to accommodate the unique requirements of vector-oriented computations, including distance calculations, similarity searches, and high-dimensional data processing.

By integrating these specialized features into the core architecture, vector databases provide a framework for implementing and executing advanced AI algorithms effectively.

This strategic alignment with the requirements of AI-driven applications distinguishes vector databases as a preferred choice for organizations seeking robust and scalable solutions for data analytics and machine learning.

In conclusion, the architecture of vector databases embodies a sophisticated blend of indexing mechanisms, data storage strategies, and retrieval processes optimized for handling vector data efficiently.

These architectural elements collectively contribute to the suitability of vector databases for AI applications and big data analytics by enabling rapid data access, processing, and analysis.

By understanding the foundational elements underlying the architecture of vector databases, organizations and data professionals can leverage these technologies to harness the power of AI-driven insights and advancements in machine learning.

Chapter 3: Indexing and Searching

Indexing in VDBs

The role of indexing in vector database efficiency

Indexing strategies play a crucial role in determining the efficiency and performance of vector databases, especially when dealing with large datasets.

These strategies are essential for facilitating fast and accurate search capabilities, enabling users to retrieve relevant information swiftly.

One common approach used in vector databases is the use of approximate nearest neighbor (ANN) algorithms for indexing.

ANN algorithms offer a balance between search speed and accuracy, making them ideal for applications where exact matches are not required.

By pre-computing approximate nearest neighbors for query vectors, indexing significantly reduces the search space, leading to faster query processing times and improved database performance.

Moreover, the choice of indexing strategy can heavily impact the scalability of a vector database.

Scalability is crucial for handling increasing volumes of data and maintaining optimal performance as the dataset grows.

Different indexing techniques have varying degrees of scalability, with some being better suited for larger datasets or high-dimensional data.

For instance, tree-based indexing structures like KD-trees or ball trees are commonly used for ANN search in high-dimensional spaces due to their efficiency in narrowing down search candidates.

On the other hand, graph-based indexing methods such as Graph Index Nearest Neighbor (GINN) offer advantages in terms of scalability and adaptability to dynamic datasets.

However, selecting an indexing strategy involves trade-offs between factors like search speed, accuracy, index size, and update complexity.

For example, while ANN algorithms provide rapid search capabilities, they may sacrifice some accuracy compared to exact neighbor searches.

Additionally, maintaining the index structures and updating them as new data points are added can incur overhead costs in terms of storage and computational resources.

It's essential for database architects and engineers specializing in vector databases to carefully evaluate these trade-offs based on the specific requirements of their applications.

By understanding the impact of indexing strategies on database performance and scalability, they can make informed decisions to optimize query efficiency and overall system performance.

Chapter 4: Indexing and Searching

Searching Mechanisms

Understanding search mechanisms in vector databases

Searching mechanisms in vector databases play a crucial role in efficiently retrieving relevant data from large datasets.

One of the fundamental searching mechanisms is the brute force search method, which involves comparing the query vector with every vector in the database to find the closest match.

While this approach is simple and easy to implement, it can be computationally expensive, especially for high-dimensional datasets.

As such, more advanced and efficient searching techniques have been developed to address this challenge.

One of the key advancements in search mechanisms for vector databases is the use of Approximate Nearest Neighbor (ANN) searching.

ANN algorithms, such as locality-sensitive hashing (LSH) and hierarchical navigable small world graphs (HNSW), offer a more efficient way to find approximate nearest neighbors without the need to compare the query vector with every vector in the database.

These algorithms use different strategies to partition the data space and navigate through it to locate the nearest neighbors, significantly reducing the search time while maintaining an acceptable level of accuracy.

Another important searching mechanism is the k-d tree, which is a data structure that organizes points in a multi-dimensional space.

By recursively partitioning the space into smaller regions, the k-d tree facilitates faster searching by narrowing down the search space based on the query vector's proximity to various partitioning planes.

This approach is particularly effective for low-dimensional datasets, where the search complexity can be reduced compared to brute force methods.

Additionally, tree-based structures like the k-d tree can be combined with ANN algorithms to further improve search efficiency and accuracy in high-dimensional spaces.

In practical terms, these searching mechanisms in vector databases enable a wide range of applications in real-world scenarios.

From recommendation systems to image and video retrieval, the ability to quickly and accurately search for similar vectors within large datasets is essential for enhancing user experiences and optimizing data analytics processes.

By understanding and implementing these advanced search mechanisms, AI/ML engineers and architects specializing in vector databases can unlock the full potential of their data analytics solutions, leading to improved performance, scalability, and competitiveness in the field.

Chapter 5: Scaling Vector Databases

Scaling Challenges

Identifying and addressing scaling challenges

Vector databases present unique challenges as they scale up to meet the demands of modern data analytics applications.

One of the main challenges in scaling vector databases is maintaining optimal performance as the size of the database grows.

As the volume of data increases, queries and operations on the database can slow down, impacting overall system efficiency.

To address this challenge, AI/ML Engineers or Architects specializing in vector databases must implement strategies such as query optimization, indexing, and efficient storage mechanisms to ensure that performance remains consistent even with large datasets.

Another key challenge in scaling vector databases is ensuring data consistency across distributed systems.

In a distributed environment, where data is spread across multiple nodes or servers, maintaining consistency can be complex.

Inconsistent data can lead to errors, inaccuracies, or discrepancies in query results, compromising the integrity of the database.

To tackle this challenge, engineers can employ techniques like replication, versioning, and synchronization mechanisms to synchronize data across all nodes and guarantee consistency at any scale.

Implementing robust data consistency mechanisms is crucial for the reliability and accuracy of the database as it grows in size and complexity.

Additionally, scalability challenges in vector databases often involve designing and implementing effective distributed architectures and load balancing strategies.

Distributed architectures allow for horizontal scaling by adding more nodes to the database system, enabling it to handle increased workloads and growing data volumes.

However, maintaining balance and efficiency across these distributed nodes is essential to prevent bottlenecks, uneven utilization of resources, and potential performance issues.

Engineers must carefully plan and implement load balancing techniques to evenly distribute query processing and data storage tasks among nodes, optimizing resource usage and system performance.

By addressing these scaling challenges proactively, AI/ML Engineers can build robust and scalable vector database solutions that meet the evolving needs of data analytics applications.

Chapter 6: Scaling Vector Databases

Distributed VDBs

Exploring distributed architectures for VDBs

The scalability of vector databases, a critical component in modern data analytics, can be significantly enhanced through distributed architectures.

By exploring the principles behind distributed vector databases, including key concepts such as data partitioning, replication, and consistency models, we can gain insights into how these systems operate efficiently in distributed environments.

One of the fundamental principles behind distributed vector databases is data partitioning.

In this technique, the database is divided into smaller, manageable parts, known as partitions, which are spread across multiple servers or nodes within a network.

This partitioning allows for parallel processing of queries and operations, enabling faster data retrieval and analysis.

Replication is another essential principle in distributed vector databases.

By replicating data across multiple nodes, these databases can ensure fault tolerance and high availability.

In the event of a node failure, data can be retrieved from replicated copies, minimizing downtime and data loss.

Furthermore, consistency models play a crucial role in distributed architectures for vector databases.

These models define how and when data updates are propagated across the network, ensuring that all nodes have access to the most recent and consistent data.

By implementing appropriate consistency models, distributed vector databases can maintain data integrity and reliability across the system.

In summary, exploring distributed architectures for vector databases is essential for achieving optimal scalability, fault tolerance, and efficiency in data analytics operations.

By understanding the key principles of data partitioning, replication, and consistency models, AI/ML engineers and architects specializing in vector databases can design and deploy scalable solutions that meet the growing demands of modern data-driven applications.

Leveraging distributed architectures allows for parallel processing, fault tolerance, and consistent data access, making distributed vector databases a powerful tool for handling large-scale data analytics tasks in cloud environments.

Chapter 7: Scaling Vector Databases

Cloud-based VDBs

Advantages of cloud solutions for VDBs

Cloud solutions play a crucial role in enhancing the deployment of vector databases, offering a range of advantages for organizations looking to leverage the power of data analytics effectively.

One of the primary benefits of using cloud platforms for vector database deployments is scalability.

Cloud services allow for the quick and efficient scaling of resources based on demand, enabling businesses to handle varying workloads without the need for substantial upfront investments in infrastructure.

This flexibility is especially valuable for organizations dealing with fluctuating data volumes or seasonal peaks, as they can easily allocate additional resources as needed without worrying about hardware limitations.

Furthermore, cloud solutions contribute to cost-effectiveness in deploying vector databases.

By utilizing cloud services, organizations can avoid the significant costs associated with setting up and maintaining on-premises infrastructure.

Cloud providers typically offer pay-as-you-go pricing models, allowing businesses to pay only for the resources they use.

This results in lower operational expenses, as companies can benefit from economies of scale and the shared infrastructure provided by cloud vendors.

Additionally, the cloud eliminates the need for physical hardware maintenance and upgrades, further reducing overall costs and allowing organizations to allocate resources more efficiently.

In the realm of cloud-based vector databases (VDBs), it is essential to consider the different deployment models available and their respective benefits.

Public cloud services, such as Amazon Web Services (AWS) or Microsoft Azure, offer a shared infrastructure model where resources are accessed over the internet.

Private clouds, on the other hand, provide dedicated resources for single organizations and offer more control over data and security.

Hybrid cloud solutions combine aspects of both public and private clouds, allowing businesses to leverage the advantages of both models.

When choosing a cloud provider for deploying VDBs, organizations need to consider factors such as performance, security, compliance, and cost to ensure that their data analytics needs are met effectively.

In addition to leveraging traditional cloud services for deploying vector databases, organizations can also benefit from utilizing cloud-native services to enhance performance and flexibility.

Cloud-native services are designed to work seamlessly with cloud environments and offer features such as auto-scaling, high availability, and fault tolerance.

By incorporating these services into their VDB deployments, organizations can optimize performance, streamline operations, and ensure data consistency and reliability.

Moreover, cloud-native services enable businesses to take advantage of advanced capabilities such as serverless computing, containerization, and microservices architecture, empowering them to build scalable and resilient data analytics solutions that can adapt to evolving business requirements.

Chapter 8: AI/ML Integration

Integrating AI Models

Integrating AI/ML models with vector databases

Integrating AI/ML models with vector databases is a crucial aspect of leveraging the power of data analytics for real-world applications.

By incorporating pre-trained AI models into vector databases, organizations can streamline their data processing workflows and enable more efficient querying and analysis.

The process typically involves model serving, which ensures that the AI/ML models are accessible within the database environment, as well as mechanisms for updating and maintaining model accuracy over time.

One of the primary challenges in integrating AI/ML models with vector databases is the need for seamless communication between the two systems.

Ensuring that the models can be efficiently deployed and queried within the database environment requires a deep understanding of both machine learning algorithms and database management principles.

Additionally, optimizing the performance of AI/ML models within a database setting involves factors such as data normalization, feature engineering, and fine-tuning hyperparameters to achieve the desired level of accuracy and efficiency.

Moreover, maintaining the accuracy and relevance of AI/ML models over time presents another significant challenge.

As data dynamics evolve and new patterns emerge, it is essential to implement mechanisms for continuous model monitoring, retraining, and updating.

This process often involves developing robust pipelines for model versioning, tracking, and deployment, ensuring that the models deployed within vector databases remain up-to-date and reflective of the most recent data trends.

By addressing these challenges proactively, organizations can enhance the effectiveness of their data analytics initiatives and derive actionable insights from their vector database infrastructure.

Chapter 9: AI/ML Integration

Real-time Data Processing

Handling real-time data processing in VDBs

Real-time data processing in vector databases is a critical aspect for applications that require instantaneous insights and decision-making capabilities.

The strategies for handling real-time data processing in VDBs are focused on optimizing the ingestion, processing, and querying of data with minimal latency.

One key technical approach involves the implementation of efficient indexing mechanisms to enable rapid data retrieval and processing.

By strategically organizing and structuring data within the vector database, queries can be executed with high throughput and low response times, facilitating real-time data analysis.

Moreover, the utilization of distributed computing frameworks and parallel processing techniques plays a vital role in enhancing the real-time processing capabilities of vector databases.

By leveraging the parallelization of computational tasks across multiple nodes or clusters, VDBs can efficiently scale to handle large volumes of data while maintaining swift response times.

This approach also enables horizontal scalability, ensuring that the database system can seamlessly expand its processing capacity as the data load increases.

Additionally, the integration of stream processing technologies can further streamline real-time data processing in VDBs by enabling continuous data ingestion, processing, and analysis without the need for persistent storage.

The impact of real-time data processing on system architecture and resource allocation is profound in the context of vector databases.

To manage the dynamic nature of real-time data streams, VDB architectures must be designed to prioritize low-latency processing and efficient resource utilization.

This entails implementing optimized data pipelines, efficient memory management strategies, and intelligent load balancing mechanisms to ensure that real-time queries are processed swiftly and accurately.

Furthermore, the allocation of computational resources such as CPU cores, memory, and network bandwidth must be carefully orchestrated to meet the demands of real-time data processing while maintaining system stability and reliability.

By adopting a holistic approach to system design and resource planning, organizations can harness the full potential of vector databases for real-time data analytics and decision-making processes.

Chapter 10: Practical Applications

Vector-based Search

Implementing vector-based search engines

Section: Vector-based Search

Sub-Section Name: Implementing vector-based search engines

In the realm of search engine technology, vector databases play a pivotal role in powering advanced search engines through their unique capabilities in handling vector data structures.

Vector databases excel in efficiently storing and querying high-dimensional vectors, making them ideal for applications that require complex similarity searches.

These databases enable the implementation of vector-based search engines by utilizing advanced algorithms for vector similarity search and ranking.

By leveraging the intrinsic properties of vectors, such as magnitude and direction, these search engines can provide more accurate and relevant results compared to traditional keyword-based search approaches.

One of the key benefits of implementing vector-based search engines lies in their ability to enhance search accuracy and relevance.

Traditional search engines often rely on keyword matching, which can lead to imprecise results and irrelevant content being retrieved.

In contrast, vector-based search engines use sophisticated algorithms to calculate similarity between vectors, enabling them to deliver more precise search results based on semantic and contextual relevance.

This results in a more personalized and efficient search experience for users, as the search engine can better understand the underlying relationships and similarities between different data points.

Moreover, vector-based search engines offer scalability and performance advantages, particularly in handling large volumes of data and complex queries.

By efficiently indexing and retrieving vectors, these search engines can quickly process search requests and provide real-time results even with vast amounts of data.

This scalability is crucial for businesses and organizations dealing with big data analytics or complex search requirements.

Additionally, vector-based search engines can improve user engagement and satisfaction by presenting results in a more intuitive and structured manner, enhancing the overall user experience and facilitating quicker decision-making processes.

In conclusion, the emergence of vector databases and their integration into search engine technology have opened up new possibilities for advanced search capabilities.

By harnessing the power of vectors and leveraging sophisticated algorithms for similarity search, vector-based search engines offer unparalleled accuracy, relevance, and scalability compared to traditional search methodologies.

As organizations continue to prioritize data analytics and information retrieval, adopting vector-based search engines can significantly enhance their search capabilities and drive innovation in the field of data analytics and search technology.

Chapter 11: Practical Applications

Recommender Systems with VDBs

Crafting recommendation systems using VDBs

Recommender Systems with VDBs: Crafting Personalized Recommendations

Vector databases play a crucial role in the development of recommendation systems, particularly in the area of crafting personalized and dynamic recommendations to users.

These systems leverage the power of vector representations of users and items to understand preferences, similarities, and patterns in user behavior.

By utilizing vector databases, recommendation engines can efficiently process and store these high-dimensional vectors, enabling quick retrieval and computation of recommendations in real-time.

The ability to handle complex mathematical computations on vector data sets is essential for providing accurate and relevant recommendations to users in diverse application domains such as e-commerce, content streaming platforms, and social networks.

One key challenge that vector databases address in recommendation systems is the need for scalability and responsiveness.

As recommendation engines deal with vast amounts of user and item data, the storage and retrieval of vector representations can become computationally intensive.

Vector databases are designed to efficiently handle high-dimensional data, making it easier to scale the system as the user base grows and ensuring that recommendations are generated promptly.

Moreover, the distributed nature of many vector database architectures allows for parallel processing of recommendation tasks, further enhancing system responsiveness and performance.

Successful implementation of recommendation systems with vector databases requires a comprehensive understanding of both the underlying algorithms and the database management aspects.

Machine learning algorithms, such as collaborative filtering or matrix factorization, are commonly used in recommendation systems to generate user and item vectors.

These vectors are stored and managed in vector databases, which must be optimized for fast retrieval and query processing.

Additionally, integrating vector databases with cloud platforms can enhance scalability and provide access to resources for deploying and maintaining scalable recommendation systems.

Continuous monitoring and optimization of the system architecture are essential to ensure that the recommendation engine remains effective and up-to-date with evolving user preferences and trends.

In conclusion, leveraging vector databases in recommendation systems is crucial for crafting personalized and dynamic recommendations that meet the increasing demands of users for relevant and engaging content.

By utilizing the capabilities of vector databases to process and store high-dimensional vectors efficiently, recommendation engines can overcome scalability and responsiveness challenges, providing timely recommendations to users.

As AI/ML Engineers or Architects specializing in vector databases, continuous learning and staying updated with the latest advancements in ML algorithms, database management, and cloud technologies are essential for designing and deploying successful recommendation systems that drive user engagement and satisfaction.

Chapter 12: Advanced Techniques

ANN Search Algorithms

Diving deep into ANN search algorithms

Sub-Section Name: ANN Search Algorithms

Approximate Nearest Neighbor (ANN) search algorithms are essential components when it comes to optimizing the performance and efficiency of vector databases.

These algorithms are designed to quickly identify the nearest neighbors of a given vector within a dataset, without requiring an exhaustive search through the entire dataset.

ANN search algorithms play a crucial role in various data-intensive applications, such as recommendation systems, image retrieval, and natural language processing.

By understanding the underlying principles and practical applications of ANN algorithms, AI/ML engineers and architects can significantly enhance the scalability and speed of their data analytics solutions.

One of the fundamental ANN search algorithms is the Locality-Sensitive Hashing (LSH) technique, which aims to hash vectors in a way that similar vectors are mapped to the same bucket with high probability.

LSH significantly reduces the search space for nearest neighbor queries, making it a popular choice for high-dimensional data.

Another notable algorithm is the KD-tree, which recursively partitions the dataset based on the median value of a selected dimension.

KD-trees are efficient for low-dimensional data but may suffer from performance degradation in high-dimensional spaces due to the curse of dimensionality.

Additionally, the Hierarchical Navigable Small World (HNSW) algorithm leverages graph-based data structures to build a navigable network for fast neighbor search.

Performance considerations are crucial when selecting the most suitable ANN algorithm for a specific use case.

Factors such as dataset dimensionality, dataset size, and query latency requirements should all be taken into account.

Engineers should also consider trade-offs between accuracy and speed, as some algorithms may prioritize faster search times at the expense of slightly reduced accuracy.

Experimentation and benchmarking different ANN algorithms on representative datasets can help in identifying the optimal solution for a particular application.

Overall, an in-depth understanding of ANN search algorithms is indispensable for AI/ML engineers and architects specializing in vector databases, allowing them to design efficient and scalable data analytics solutions that meet the needs of modern data-driven industries.

Chapter 13: Advanced Techniques

Optimizing VDB Performance

Strategies for optimizing vector database performance

Optimizing VDB Performance: Strategies for Enhancing Efficiency

Optimizing the performance of vector databases plays a crucial role in achieving efficient data analytics and processing.

To navigate the future of data analytics effectively, AI/ML Engineers specializing in vector databases must implement key strategies aimed at enhancing database efficiency.

One of the primary strategies for optimizing vector database performance involves indexing optimizations.

By creating appropriate indexes on the vectors, the retrieval and search operations can be significantly accelerated.

This technique not only improves the speed of data access but also enhances the overall query performance.

Another essential strategy for optimizing vector database performance is query optimization.

By carefully structuring queries, utilizing efficient search algorithms, and minimizing unnecessary data retrieval, AI/ML Engineers can reduce query processing time and enhance database responsiveness.

Query optimization is a continuous process that involves analyzing query execution plans, identifying bottlenecks, and fine-tuning the database configuration for optimal performance.

Through effective query optimization techniques, vector databases can deliver faster results and improved scalability, making them ideal for handling large volumes of multidimensional data.

Furthermore, leveraging GPU acceleration is a cutting-edge strategy for optimizing vector database performance.

Graphics Processing Units (GPUs) are highly efficient in parallel processing tasks, making them well-suited for accelerating complex data computations in vector databases.

By harnessing the computational power of GPUs, AI/ML Engineers can achieve significant performance gains in tasks such as similarity search, clustering, and dimensionality reduction.

Integrating GPU acceleration into the database architecture requires specialized knowledge and expertise but can result in substantial speed improvements and scalability enhancements, especially in AI applications requiring real-time processing capabilities.

In conclusion, optimizing the performance of vector databases is a multifaceted process that demands a combination of hardware enhancements, algorithmic improvements, and strategic optimizations.

By implementing indexing optimizations, query optimization techniques, and leveraging GPU acceleration, AI/ML Engineers can unlock the full potential of vector databases and navigate the future of data analytics with greater efficiency and effectiveness.

Continuous learning, experimentation, and staying abreast of advancements in the field are essential for professionals in this domain to drive innovation and deliver high-performance scalable solutions in the rapidly evolving landscape of artificial intelligence and machine learning.

Chapter 14: Emerging Technologies

Quantum Computing & VDBs

The potential impact of quantum computing on VDBs

As a visionary in the field of AI/ML engineering and architecture, especially specializing in vector databases, it is imperative to explore the potential impact of quantum computing on the future of this technology.

Quantum computing is set to revolutionize various sectors, and its integration with vector databases opens up new horizons for advanced data analytics.

Traditional computing methods are reaching their limits in handling complex data structures efficiently, making the introduction of quantum algorithms a promising avenue to enhance database operations, particularly in the realms of search and optimization processes.

Quantum computing possesses the remarkable ability to process vast amounts of data simultaneously by leveraging quantum bits or qubits, as opposed to classical bits that can only exist in a state of 0 or 1.

This quantum parallelism introduces a paradigm shift in how computations are performed, potentially enabling vector databases to handle massive datasets with enhanced speed and efficiency.

By harnessing the power of quantum algorithms, such as Grover's algorithm for search optimization, vector databases can significantly accelerate search queries and streamline data retrieval processes.

This optimization can lead to faster decision-making, predictive modeling, and overall improved performance of vector databases.

Moreover, quantum computing's inherent nature of entanglement and superposition can offer novel solutions to the challenges faced by current database technologies.

The principles of entanglement allow qubits to be interconnected in a way that their states are dependent on each other, leading to the potential for distributed parallel processing and enhanced data correlation within vector databases.

Additionally, superposition enables qubits to exist in multiple states simultaneously, opening up possibilities for more sophisticated data representation and storage methods within vector databases.

With the integration of quantum computing, vector databases can evolve to efficiently process high-dimensional data and complex relationships, thereby advancing the frontiers of data analytics and machine learning capabilities.

In conclusion, the fusion of quantum computing with vector databases presents an exciting future for data analytics, offering unparalleled opportunities for innovation and advancements in the field.

By harnessing quantum algorithms and leveraging the unique properties of quantum computing, such as superposition and entanglement, vector databases can enhance their performance, scalability, and efficiency.

As an aspiring AI/ML engineer or architect specializing in vector databases, staying abreast of the developments in quantum computing and its potential impact on database technologies is essential for driving future growth and success in the realm of advanced data analytics.

Chapter 15: Emerging Technologies

Integration with Graph DBs

Integrating vector and graph databases for advanced analytics

Integrating vector and graph databases for advanced analytics involves combining the strengths of both types of databases to extract deeper insights from complex data structures.

Graph databases excel at representing and analyzing relationships between entities, making them ideal for scenarios such as social network analysis, fraud detection, and recommendation systems.

On the other hand, vector databases are powerful at capturing numerical representations of data points in high-dimensional spaces, enabling efficient similarity search and clustering tasks.

By integrating these two technologies, organizations can leverage the strengths of each to drive innovation and enhance their analytical capabilities.

One key benefit of integrating vector and graph databases is the ability to uncover latent relationships and patterns in data that might be challenging to identify using traditional methods.

Vector databases store data points in mathematical vector representations, allowing for quick similarity searches and nearest neighbor queries.

When combined with graph databases, which focus on capturing complex relationships between entities, organizations can gain a more comprehensive understanding of their data ecosystem.

This integrated approach enables companies to discover hidden correlations, anomalies, and trends that can be vital for making informed business decisions and detecting emerging patterns.

Moreover, the integration of vector and graph databases facilitates more sophisticated and context-aware analytics by providing a holistic view of the data landscape.

For instance, in the realm of content recommendation systems, combining vector representations of user preferences with graph structures of content relationships can enhance the accuracy and relevance of personalized recommendations.

By leveraging the strengths of both vector and graph databases, organizations can create more robust and adaptive analytics solutions that adapt to changing user preferences and behavior patterns.

This fusion of technologies opens up new possibilities for delivering more intelligent and dynamic services to end-users.

In conclusion, the integration of vector and graph databases represents a powerful approach to unlocking the full potential of data analytics and content insights.

By combining the strengths of vector databases in processing high-dimensional numerical data with the relationship-centric capabilities of graph databases, organizations can enrich their analysis, uncover hidden patterns, and drive innovation in their operations.

Practical examples and use cases demonstrate the transformative impact of this integration, showcasing how companies can leverage advanced analytics to gain a competitive edge in today's data-driven landscape.

As organizations continue to seek more sophisticated ways to extract value from their data, the convergence of vector and graph databases stands out as a key enabler for advanced analytics and informed decision-making.

Chapter 16: Case Studies

Search in E-commerce

Enhancing e-commerce search with vector databases

Enhancing E-commerce Search with Vector Databases

In the fast-evolving realm of e-commerce, the ability to provide a seamless and intuitive search experience for customers is paramount.

Leveraging vector databases in enhancing e-commerce search functionalities has emerged as a game-changer, revolutionizing how businesses interact with their customers online.

By representing data points as vectors in multidimensional space, vector databases enable advanced similarity searches, resulting in more accurate and relevant product recommendations tailored to individual user preferences.

Technical Implementation and Challenges

The integration of vector databases into e-commerce platforms involves a sophisticated blend of data engineering, machine learning algorithms, and database management.

One of the key technical aspects is encoding product attributes and user behavior into high-dimensional vectors to enable efficient similarity computations.

This process requires expertise in deploying ML models for feature extraction and vectorization, ensuring that the underlying data representation captures the nuances of user intent effectively.

However, challenges may arise in managing the high dimensionality of vector representations, as well as optimizing query performance to deliver real-time search results that meet user expectations.

Impact on Business Metrics

The adoption of vector databases in e-commerce search has yielded significant improvements in key business metrics, driving enhanced product discovery and ultimately, customer satisfaction.

By enabling more personalized search results based on user preferences and behavioral patterns, businesses can increase user engagement, conversion rates, and customer retention.

Furthermore, the ability to scale search capabilities seamlessly with vector databases empowers e-commerce platforms to handle increasing volumes of data and user interactions, ensuring a robust and responsive search experience even during peak traffic periods.

In essence, the transformative impact of vector databases on e-commerce search functionality underscores their role as a cornerstone of modern data analytics in the digital marketplace.

In conclusion, the case study on the impact of vector databases on e-commerce search functionality highlights the transformative potential of leveraging advanced data analytics technologies to enhance customer experiences and drive business growth.

Through a strategic integration of vector databases into e-commerce platforms, businesses can unlock the power of data-driven insights to deliver personalized and efficient search results, ultimately setting new standards for online retail in the digital age.

As the landscape of e-commerce continues to evolve, embracing the future of data analytics through vector databases is not only a competitive advantage but a necessity for staying ahead in a dynamic and customer-centric marketplace.

Chapter 17: Case Studies

Content Discovery

Content discovery in media and entertainment

As an AI/ML engineer or architect specializing in vector databases, you would possess a comprehensive understanding of how these databases play a vital role in powering content discovery engines in the media and entertainment industry.

One key aspect in which vector databases excel is content recommendation, where algorithms are leveraged to enhance user experience by offering personalized suggestions based on preferences and viewing patterns.

By utilizing vector databases, media companies can efficiently store and retrieve high-dimensional data representations of content items, enabling quicker and more accurate recommendations to users.

In a case study focused on content discovery in media and entertainment, the implementation of vecto databases for content recommendation would involve the selection and optimization of machine learning algorithms tailored to the specific needs of the platform.

These algorithms would be designed to process vast amounts of user interaction data, such as viewing history, ratings, and preferences, to create meaningful embeddings that represent each user and content item in a high-dimensional space.

The scalability challenges in this context would revolve around handling the large volumes of data generated by user interactions and ensuring that the database can efficiently support real-time queryin and updating to deliver timely recommendations.

The outcomes achieved by implementing vector databases for content recommendation in media and entertainment would be measured in terms of user engagement and content relevancy.

By leveraging advanced algorithms and efficient database management techniques, media companies can enhance user satisfaction through personalized content suggestions that align with individual preferences.

Improved content relevancy leads to higher user retention rates, increased platform engagement, and ultimately, a competitive edge in the market.

Overall, the successful deployment of vector databases for content discovery can revolutionize the way media and entertainment platforms cater to user needs, offering a rich and dynamic viewing experienc that keeps audiences coming back for more.

Chapter 18: Security and Privacy

Security Best Practices

Best practices for securing vector databases

Security Best Practices for Vector Databases

Ensuring the security of vector databases is a critical aspect of database management, particularly in contexts where sensitive data is involved.

Implementing robust security measures is essential to safeguard the integrity and confidentiality of data stored within these databases.

One of the foundational best practices for securing vector databases is data encryption.

By encrypting data at rest and in transit, you can protect it from unauthorized access and ensure that even if a breach occurs, the data remains unintelligible to any malicious actors.

Utilizing strong encryption algorithms and key management practices is imperative to prevent data breaches and maintain data privacy.

Access control is another key aspect of securing vector databases.

Implementing granular access controls ensures that only authorized users can access specific data within the database.

Role-based access control (RBAC) and attribute-based access control (ABAC) are commonly used techniques to restrict access based on user roles and data attributes.

By defining and enforcing access policies, you can mitigate the risk of unauthorized access and data leakage.

It is also advisable to regularly review and update access controls to align with organizational changes and maintain the principle of least privilege.

Network security measures play a crucial role in securing vector databases, especially in distributed or cloud-based environments.

Employing secure communication protocols such as SSL/TLS for data transmission between clients and servers helps prevent eavesdropping and data interception.

Implementing firewalls, intrusion detection systems, and network segmentation techniques can further enhance the security posture of the database infrastructure.

Regular network vulnerability assessments and penetration testing are essential to identify and remediate potential security gaps before they are exploited by malicious actors.

In addition to encryption, access controls, and network security, a comprehensive security strategy for vector databases should also include regular security audits and compliance checks.

Conducting periodic security assessments helps identify vulnerabilities and gaps in the security posture of the database environment.

Compliance with data protection regulations such as GDPR, HIPAA, or PCI DSS is crucial for organizations handling sensitive data.

By staying informed about emerging security threats and best practices, AI/ML Engineers or Architects specializing in vector databases can effectively safeguard data assets and maintain trust with stakeholders.

Remember to cite any sources you've referred to in the content.

Chapter 19: Security and Privacy

Privacy in AI Applications

Ensuring data privacy in AI applications using VDBs

Privacy in AI Applications

Data privacy is a paramount concern in the realm of artificial intelligence (AI) and machine learning (ML) applications, particularly when utilizing vector databases (VDBs). VDBs play a crucial role in storing and manipulating high-dimensional and complex data structures, making them a fundamental component in various AI-driven projects.

Nevertheless, the use of VDBs introduces new challenges in terms of maintaining the privacy of sensitive information.

To safeguard data privacy in AI applications that leverage VDBs, it is essential to implement robust strategies and measures that comply with regulatory requirements and ensure the confidentiality of personal data.

One of the key considerations in maintaining data privacy in AI applications using VDBs is to adhere to relevant regulations and standards.

Data privacy laws such as the General Data Protection Regulation (GDPR) and the California Consumer Privacy Act (CCPA) impose stringent requirements on how organizations handle and protect personal data.

AI engineers and architects specializing in VDBs must stay informed about these regulations and ensure that their solutions adhere to the stipulated guidelines, including data minimization, purpose limitation, and the right to erasure.

By incorporating privacy-by-design principles into the development process, practitioners can proactively address privacy concerns and mitigate the risks associated with data misuse.

In addition to regulatory compliance, anonymization techniques play a crucial role in preserving data privacy when working with VDBs in AI applications.

Anonymization involves removing identifying information from datasets to prevent the re-identification of individuals.

Common anonymization methods include generalization, perturbation, and masking, which help anonymize sensitive attributes without compromising data utility.

By anonymizing data before storing it in VDBs, organizations can minimize the risk of privacy breaches while still leveraging the power of AI for insights and decision-making.

However, it is essential to strike a balance between anonymization and data quality to ensure that the anonymized data remains useful for analytical purposes.

Moreover, the use of privacy-preserving algorithms can further enhance data privacy in AI applications utilizing VDBs.

These algorithms enable computations to be performed on encrypted data without revealing the underlying information, thereby protecting sensitive data from unauthorized access.

Techniques such as homomorphic encryption, secure multiparty computation, and differential privacy offer innovative ways to ensure privacy in AI workflows without compromising the accuracy of ML models.

By integrating privacy-preserving algorithms into their systems, AI engineers can build trust with users and stakeholders by demonstrating a strong commitment to data privacy and security.

Chapter 20: Industry Impacts

Personalized Medicine

Personalizing medicine with vector databases

The future of personalized medicine is being significantly shaped by the advent of vector databases, which play a pivotal role in enabling the analysis of vast amounts of biomedical data.

Personalized medicine, at its core, aims to tailor healthcare decisions and medical treatments to individual characteristics, such as genetic makeup, lifestyle, and environmental factors.

Vector databases offer a sophisticated framework for storing, organizing, and querying complex data structures, particularly in the realms of genomics, drug discovery, and patient data analysis.

In genomics, vector databases are instrumental in managing the enormous volumes of genetic information generated through various sequencing technologies.

These databases allow researchers and clinicians to efficiently analyze and interpret genetic data, identifying patterns, mutations, and associations that can inform personalized treatment strategies.

By leveraging machine learning algorithms within vector databases, researchers can uncover valuable insights into the genetic basis of diseases, leading to the development of targeted therapies and interventions tailored to individual patients.

When it comes to drug discovery, vector databases provide a powerful platform for storing molecular structures, chemical properties, and biological interactions of potential drug candidates.

By integrating diverse datasets within a unified vector database architecture, researchers can accelerate the identification of novel drug targets, predict drug efficacy, and optimize treatment regimens based on individual patient profiles.

This data-driven approach to drug development is revolutionizing precision medicine, enabling the design of tailored therapies that improve outcomes and minimize adverse effects.

Moreover, in patient data analysis, vector databases offer a comprehensive solution for integrating clinical records, imaging data, biomarker profiles, and treatment outcomes.

By structuring patient data in a vector format, healthcare providers can perform rapid searches, correlations, and predictive modeling to deliver personalized care pathways.

From risk assessment to treatment selection, vector databases empower clinicians with evidence-based insights and decision support tools that enhance the quality of care and patient outcomes.

In essence, vector databases are not just shaping the future of personalized medicine—they are redefining the landscape of healthcare by unlocking the full potential of data analytics and artificial intelligence in driving precision healthcare initiatives.

Chapter 21: Industry Impacts

Fraud Detection

Enhancing fraud detection with vector databases

Vector databases play a crucial role in enhancing fraud detection in the finance sector by significantly improving the efficiency and accuracy of fraud detection systems.

These databases are designed to handle high-dimensional data efficiently, making them ideal for processing vast amounts of transactional data in real-time.

By leveraging advanced machine learning algorithms and in-memory computing capabilities, vector databases can quickly analyze complex patterns and relationships within financial data to identify potential fraudulent activities.

One key advantage of using vector databases for fraud detection in finance is their ability to perform in-depth analysis of transactional data to detect anomalies and suspicious activities.

Traditional databases often struggle to handle the sheer volume and complexity of financial data, leading to delays in identifying fraudulent transactions.

In contrast, vector databases are highly optimized for processing high-dimensional data, allowing them to detect outliers and patterns indicative of fraud with greater speed and accuracy.

Furthermore, the use of vector databases enables financial institutions to adapt quickly to evolving fraud tactics and patterns.

By continuously analyzing and learning from historical data, these databases can constantly improve their fraud detection models to stay ahead of sophisticated fraudsters.

This adaptive nature is crucial in the fast-paced world of finance, where new fraud schemes emerge regularly, and traditional detection methods may fall short.

With vector databases, financial institutions can enhance their fraud detection capabilities by leveraging advanced analytics to detect even the most subtle indicators of fraudulent activities.

In conclusion, the application of vector databases in fraud detection systems within the finance sector represents a significant leap forward in combating financial fraud.

By harnessing the power of high-dimensional data processing, machine learning algorithms, and real-time analytics, these databases empower financial institutions to detect and prevent fraudulent activities more effectively than ever before.

As the landscape of financial fraud continues to evolve, the use of vector databases will be crucial in ensuring that fraud detection systems remain robust, efficient, and adaptive to emerging threats, ultimately safeguarding the integrity of financial transactions and protecting both institutions and consumers from financial harm.

Chapter 22: Performance Tuning

Query Optimization Techniques

Optimizing queries in vector databases for performance

Query optimization in vector databases plays a crucial role in enhancing performance and content retrieval efficiency.

To achieve optimal query performance, advanced strategies need to be employed, focusing on reducing latency and improving accuracy.

One key aspect of query optimization in vector databases is query planning.

This involves analyzing the query structure, data distribution, and indexing techniques to determine the most efficient execution plan.

By understanding the data characteristics and access patterns, a well-designed query plan can significantly reduce query execution time and resource consumption.

In addition to query planning, execution strategies play a vital role in optimizing queries in vector databases.

Efficient execution strategies involve leveraging parallel processing, query caching, and intelligent query processing techniques to enhance performance.

Parallel processing can be utilized to distribute query workload across multiple nodes or processors, enabling faster query execution by harnessing the computational power of multiple resources in parallel.

Query caching can also be beneficial in improving query response time by storing and reusing previously executed query results, reducing the need for redundant computations.

Furthermore, tuning performance based on specific use cases and data characteristics is essential for optimizing queries in vector databases.

Different use cases may require tailored optimization techniques to achieve the best results.

For example, queries that involve complex mathematical operations or distance computations may benefit from specialized algorithms or data structures designed to accelerate such computations.

Understanding the data distribution, dimensionality, and sparsity characteristics of the vector data can also guide the selection of appropriate indexing techniques and query optimization strategies.

In conclusion, advanced strategies for query optimization in vector databases are essential for achieving high performance and accuracy in data retrieval tasks.

By focusing on query planning, execution strategies, and tuning performance based on specific use cases and data characteristics, AI/ML engineers and architects can unlock the full potential of vector databases for advanced analytics and machine learning applications.

Continuous learning and exploration of new optimization techniques are key to staying competitive in the rapidly evolving field of data analytics and AI.

Chapter 23: Performance Tuning

Using Hardware Acceleration

Exploiting hardware acceleration for VDBs

Using Hardware Acceleration in Vector Databases

In the realm of vector databases, exploiting hardware acceleration such as GPUs (Graphics Processing Units) and TPUs (Tensor Processing Units) can yield substantial advancements in performance.

These specialized hardware components are designed to handle complex mathematical computations inherent in machine learning algorithms and data processing tasks.

When integrated adeptly, GPUs and TPUs can offer a significant boost in processing speeds and efficiency for vector databases, unlocking new possibilities for data analytics and insights.

One key consideration when harnessing hardware acceleration for vector databases is the seamless integration of these components with existing infrastructure and systems.

This involves optimizing software layers to effectively leverage the parallel processing capabilities of GPUs and TPUs.

By ensuring that data is structured and processed in a compatible manner, organizations can fully exploit the potential performance gains offered by these hardware accelerators.

Furthermore, deploying specialized frameworks and libraries that are tailored for GPU/TPU utilization can streamline the implementation process and maximize the benefits of hardware acceleration.

Despite the clear advantages of using GPUs and TPUs for enhancing vector database performance, potential bottlenecks may arise if not carefully addressed.

These bottlenecks could stem from inefficient data transfer between the CPU and GPU/TPU, suboptimal utilization of hardware resources, or inadequate synchronization of computation tasks.

To mitigate these challenges, AI/ML engineers and architects specializing in vector databases must conduct thorough performance profiling and optimization to identify and resolve bottlenecks effectively.

By fine-tuning the system configuration and workload distribution, it is possible to achieve optimal performance gains from hardware acceleration.

Real-world case studies serve as compelling evidence of the transformative impact of hardware acceleration on vector database performance.

Organizations across various industries have reported significant speed-ups in query processing, model training, and overall data analytics tasks by harnessing the computational power of GPUs and TPUs.

By showcasing these success stories, experts in the field can underscore the tangible benefits of leveraging hardware acceleration for vector databases, inspiring further innovation and adoption in the realm of data analytics and machine learning.

Chapter 24: Data Management

Efficient Data Ingestion

Strategies for efficient data ingestion into VDBs

Efficient data ingestion is a crucial aspect of managing vector databases, as it directly impacts the performance and scalability of the system.

When it comes to handling large volumes of vector data, various strategies can be employed to ensure smooth and efficient ingestion.

One common approach is batch processing, where data is collected and loaded in predefined intervals.

This method is suitable for scenarios where data updates are not required in real-time and can handle significant volumes of data at once.

Batch processing allows for the optimization of resources and can be scheduled during off-peak times to minimize disruptions to normal operations.

Another key strategy for efficient data ingestion into vector databases is stream processing.

Stream processing involves the continuous ingestion of data in real-time, allowing for immediate updates and responses to changing data.

This method is ideal for applications that require up-to-date information and can handle high-throughput data streams efficiently.

Stream processing enables faster decision-making and real-time analytics, making it a valuable tool for use cases such as real-time monitoring, fraud detection, and IoT applications.

Implementing stream processing requires careful consideration of system architecture, data flow, and processing pipelines to ensure smooth and reliable operations.

In addition to batch and stream processing, efficient data ingestion into vector databases also involves overcoming data transformation challenges.

Data transformation is the process of converting and harmonizing data from various sources into a consistent format that can be stored and analyzed effectively.

This step is crucial for ensuring data quality and consistency within the database, as discrepancies or errors in the data can lead to inaccurate analytics and insights.

To address data transformation challenges, advanced techniques such as data cleaning, normalization, and feature engineering may be employed.

By implementing robust data transformation strategies, organizations can enhance the reliability and usability of their vector databases, ultimately leading to more accurate and insightful data analytics.

Chapter 25: Data Management

Data Governance in VDBs

Implementing data governance for vector databases

Implementing Data Governance for Vector Databases

Data governance is a critical component of managing and utilizing data effectively, especially in the realm of vector databases.

As an AI/ML Engineer or Architect specializing in vector databases, it is imperative to tailor data governance strategies to ensure the integrity, security, and usability of the data in these specialized databases.

To achieve this, several key principles must be considered, including data quality management, metadata management, and regulatory compliance.

Data Quality Management
One of the primary focuses of data governance for vector databases is ensuring data quality.

Given the complexity and dimensionality of the data stored in vector databases, maintaining high data quality is essential for accurate analysis and decision-making.

Implementing processes for data cleansing, normalization, and validation can help identify and correct any inconsistencies or errors in the data.

Leveraging data quality tools and techniques specific to vector data structures is crucial for upholding the reliability of the underlying data.

Additionally, establishing data quality metrics and KPIs can provide a framework for monitoring and improving data quality over time.

Metadata Management
Effective metadata management is another key aspect of data governance in vector databases.

Metadata, which provides essential information about the data stored in the database, plays a crucial role in understanding and utilizing the data effectively.

Developing a comprehensive metadata strategy tailored to the unique characteristics of vector databases is essential for enhancing data discoverability, lineage tracking, and data governance processes.

Leveraging metadata repositories and tools that support the storage and retrieval of rich metadata attributes can streamline data management activities and facilitate data governance practices within vector databases.

Regulatory Compliance
In the context of vector databases, regulatory compliance is a critical consideration for data governance.

With data privacy regulations such as GDPR and CCPA becoming increasingly stringent, ensuring compliance with data protection laws and regulations is paramount.

Implementing mechanisms for data encryption, access control, and audit trails within vector databases can help organizations adhere to regulatory requirements and protect sensitive data.

Collaborating with legal and compliance teams to establish and enforce data governance policies that align with regulatory standards is essential for mitigating legal risks and maintaining trust in the data ecosystem.

In conclusion, implementing data governance for vector databases requires a tailored approach that encompasses data quality management, metadata management, and regulatory compliance.

By prioritizing these key principles and leveraging specialized tools and techniques designed for vector data structures, organizations can uphold the integrity, security, and usability of data within their vector databases.

Continuous monitoring, evaluation, and refinement of data governance practices are necessary to adapt to evolving data landscapes and regulatory environments, ensuring that data remains a valuable asset for driving insights and innovation in the digital age.

Chapter 26: Development Practices

DevOps Practices

Integrating DevOps practices with vector database management

DevOps Practices in Vector Database Management

DevOps practices play a crucial role in the successful integration and management of vector databases.

By implementing DevOps methodologies, organizations can streamline their development processes, enhance deployment efficiency, and ensure the seamless operation of their vector databases.

One of the key components of DevOps in the context of vector databases is continuous integration/continuous deployment (CI/CD). This approach involves automating the building, testing, and deployment of database changes, allowing for faster and more reliable updates to the database schema and data.

By integrating CI/CD pipelines into the database management workflow, teams can reduce manual errors, improve collaboration between developers and operations teams, and increase the overall agility of the database development process.

Monitoring is another critical aspect of DevOps practices in vector database management.

Continuous monitoring of the database performance, availability, and security is essential for identifying and addressing issues proactively.

With real-time monitoring tools and alerting mechanisms in place, organizations can ensure the stability and reliability of their vector databases, and quickly respond to any anomalies or performance degradation.

Additionally, monitoring helps in capacity planning and optimization, as it provides valuable insights into resource utilization trends and performance bottlenecks, allowing for better decision-making and resource allocation.

Automation is a fundamental principle of DevOps that can greatly benefit vector database management.

By automating repetitive tasks such as database provisioning, configuration management, and data backups, organizations can improve operational efficiency, reduce human errors, and accelerate the overall development lifecycle.

Automation also enables teams to standardize and repeat database deployment processes, ensuring consistency and reproducibility across different environments.

Furthermore, automation facilitates scalability and elasticity, as database resources can be dynamically provisioned and de-provisioned based on workload demands, enabling organizations to adapt to changing business requirements and optimize resource utilization.

In conclusion, integrating DevOps practices in vector database management can bring numerous benefits, including increased development speed, enhanced deployment reliability, improved operational efficiency, and better overall performance of the database system.

By embracing CI/CD pipelines, monitoring tools, and automation strategies, organizations can streamlin their database workflows, reduce manual overhead, and align their development and operations teams towards a common goal of delivering high-quality, scalable database solutions.

Continuous learning and adaptation of DevOps principles are key to staying competitive in the fast-paced world of data analytics, ensuring that organizations can effectively navigate the future of data management and analytics.

Chapter 27: Development Practices

Testing VDB Applications

Testing and validating vector database applications

Testing and Validating Vector Database Applications

In the realm of AI and machine learning, having a robust testing and validation strategy is paramount when working with vector databases.

These databases, optimized for handling high-dimensional data points efficiently, present unique challenges that necessitate specialized approaches to ensure the reliability and performance of applications.

One fundamental aspect of testing vector database applications is **unit testing**, where individual components of the code are isolated and tested in controlled environments.

This helps in verifying the correctness of functionalities and detecting any potential bugs or errors early in the development cycle.

It is crucial to design unit tests that cover different data scenarios to ensure the accuracy and consistency of results.

Integration testing is another critical aspect when it comes to validating vector database applications.

This type of testing focuses on evaluating how different modules or components interact with each other within the application ecosystem.

Given the complex nature of vector databases and their role in handling large volumes of data, integration testing becomes vital to ensure seamless communication and data flow between various parts of the system.

It helps uncover any potential issues related to data integration, storage, retrieval, and processing, thereby ensuring the overall functionality of the application.

Performance benchmarking is an essential part of the testing and validation process for vector database applications.

In this phase, the goal is to assess the speed, scalability, and efficiency of the application when working with large volumes of high-dimensional data.

Performance testing helps in identifying bottlenecks, optimizing query execution times, and fine-tuning the system for optimal performance.

By conducting rigorous performance benchmarking, AI/ML engineers and architects can gain valuable insights into the application's behavior under different workloads and make informed decisions to enhance its overall efficiency and responsiveness.

Chapter 28: Future Directions

Edge Computing and VDBs

Vector databases at the edge: Opportunities and challenges

Edge computing is revolutionizing the way organizations deploy and manage vector databases, presenting a unique set of opportunities and challenges for AI/ML engineers and architects.

By bringing compute resources closer to where data is generated, edge computing enables faster processing and real-time analytics.

This proximity to the data source results in reduced latency, which is particularly critical for applications requiring immediate insights or responses.

Vector databases, known for their ability to efficiently handle high-dimensional data and complex queries, stand to benefit significantly from edge deployments.

One key opportunity of utilizing vector databases at the edge lies in enhancing operational efficiency.

By processing and storing data locally at the edge, organizations can alleviate the burden on centralized systems, reducing the volume of data that needs to be transmitted back and forth.

This localized approach not only accelerates data processing but also mitigates network congestion and bandwidth constraints.

Furthermore, it promotes better data governance and compliance by keeping sensitive information closer to its origin and minimizing data exposure during transit.

For AI/ML engineers and architects, this means designing and implementing optimized data pipelines that leverage the strengths of both edge computing and vector databases.

However, deploying vector databases at the edge also introduces a set of challenges that must be carefully navigated.

One key consideration is the need for seamless integration between edge computing infrastructure and centralized database systems.

Maintaining consistency and coherence across distributed data storage environments requires robust synchronization mechanisms and intelligent data routing strategies.

Additionally, ensuring data security and privacy becomes paramount in edge deployments, as edge devices are often more vulnerable to security breaches compared to centralized data centers.

AI/ML engineers and architects must implement robust security protocols, encryption techniques, and access controls to safeguard data integrity and confidentiality in this decentralized paradigm.

In conclusion, the symbiotic relationship between edge computing and vector databases holds immense promise for empowering organizations with agile, real-time data analytics capabilities.

By strategically leveraging the benefits of edge deployments, including reduced latency, improved operational efficiency, and enhanced data governance, AI/ML professionals can unlock a new frontier of opportunities in the realm of advanced data analytics.

However, success in this emerging landscape requires a deep understanding of both edge computing principles and vector database technologies, as well as a proactive approach to addressing the challenges of data integration, security, and scalability.

As organizations continue to embrace the agility and flexibility offered by edge computing, the role of AI/ML engineers and architects specializing in vector databases will become increasingly vital in shaping the future of data analytics.

Chapter 29: Future Directions

Data Interoperability

Ensuring data interoperability among vector databases

Data Interoperability: Ensuring Seamless Data Exchange Among Vector Databases

In the fast-evolving landscape of data analytics, the rise of vector databases has brought about a paradigm shift in how data is stored, managed, and processed.

With the proliferation of diverse database systems and data formats, ensuring interoperability among vector databases has become a pressing concern for organizations aiming to harness the true potential of their data assets.

To achieve seamless data exchange and integration across these varied data ecosystems, strategies need to be in place to address the challenges posed by disparate technologies and standards.

One key strategy for ensuring data interoperability among vector databases is the establishment and adoption of industry standards and protocols.

Standardization plays a pivotal role in facilitating communication and data exchange between different database systems, regardless of their underlying technologies.

By adhering to common protocols such as SQL or ODBC, organizations can streamline the integration process and minimize compatibility issues when working with multiple databases concurrently.

Additionally, the use of standard formats like CSV or JSON for data representation can further enhance interoperability by enabling data portability across different systems with minimal conversion efforts.

Another essential aspect to consider in enhancing data interoperability is the utilization of specialized tools and middleware that are designed to bridge the gap between heterogeneous databases.

Middleware solutions offer advanced capabilities for data transformation, synchronization, and replication, allowing for seamless integration of data streams from disparate sources.

These tools act as intermediaries that translate data formats, optimize query performance, and ensure data consistency across distributed databases.

By deploying such tools within the data architecture, organizations can achieve a higher degree of interoperability and interoperable data exchange among their vector databases.

Furthermore, adopting a holistic approach to data management and governance is paramount in ensuring long-term interoperability among vector databases.

Centralized data governance frameworks that define data standards, quality metrics, and data lineage can provide a solid foundation for maintaining data consistency and compatibility across the organization's database infrastructure.

Implementing data quality assurance processes, metadata management strategies, and data lineage tracking mechanisms can help identify and resolve data inconsistencies, thus promoting interoperability and ensuring data reliability across disparate databases.

By prioritizing data governance as a core principle, organizations can proactively address interoperability challenges and foster a more coherent data ecosystem that is conducive to seamless data exchange and integration among vector databases.

In conclusion, the imperative for ensuring data interoperability among vector databases underscores the importance of adopting a multi-faceted approach that encompasses standardization, specialized tools, and robust data governance practices.

By embracing industry standards, leveraging middleware solutions, and implementing data governance frameworks, organizations can mitigate interoperability challenges and unlock the full potential of their data assets.

As vector databases continue to shape the future of data analytics, a proactive stance towards interoperability will be essential for organizations seeking to thrive in an increasingly data-driven environment.

Chapter 30: Visualization Techniques

Visualizing Vector Data

Techniques for visualizing data in vector databases

Visualizing vector data from databases is crucial for gaining insights and extracting value from the underlying information.

There are various techniques and tools available to effectively visualize this type of data.

One common approach is dimensionality reduction, which helps in simplifying high-dimensional data into lower dimensions for better visualization.

Principal Component Analysis (PCA) and t-SNE (t-distributed stochastic neighbor embedding) are popular techniques used to reduce the dimensionality of vector data.

By plotting the transformed data in two or three dimensions, patterns and relationships can be easily identified.

Another essential technique for visualizing vector data is clustering, which groups similar data points together based on their features.

Clustering algorithms such as K-means clustering or hierarchical clustering can help in visualizing the inherent structure within the data.

Visualization tools like scatter plots, heatmaps, and dendrograms are commonly used to represent clustered data efficiently.

These visualizations can provide a clear understanding of how data points are related and clustered together based on their similarities.

In addition to dimensionality reduction and clustering, interactive visualizations play a vital role in exploring and analyzing vector data effectively.

Tools like Plotly, D3.js, or Tableau enable users to create interactive plots and dashboards, allowing for dynamic exploration of the data.

Interactive visualizations offer a more intuitive way to navigate through large datasets, making it easier to identify trends, outliers, and correlations within the vector data.

By leveraging these tools, AI/ML engineers and architects specializing in vector databases can unlock hidden patterns and insights that traditional static visualizations might overlook.

Overall, effective visualization of vector data involves a combination of techniques such as dimensionality reduction, clustering, and interactive visualization tools.

By utilizing these methods, data professionals can uncover meaningful patterns and relationships within vector databases, leading to better decision-making and optimized solutions.

It is crucial for AI/ML engineers and architects to stay updated on the latest visualization techniques and tools to stay ahead in the rapidly evolving field of data analytics.

Chapter 31: Visualization Techniques

Interactive Analysis Tools

Enabling interactive analysis with vector databases

Title: Vector Databases Unleashed: Navigating the Future of Data Analytics

Interactive Analysis Tools for Vector Databases

Interactive analysis tools play a crucial role in empowering users to delve deeper into the data stored in vector databases.

These tools enable real-time exploration and manipulation of the data, allowing for immediate insights and informed decision-making processes.

By utilizing interactive analysis tools in conjunction with vector databases, organizations can unlock the full potential of their data assets.

One of the key tools that facilitate interactive analysis of vector database data is visualization software such as Tableau, Power BI, or Grafana.

These tools provide intuitive interfaces that allow users to create interactive dashboards and visualizations, making it easier to identify patterns, trends, and outliers within the data.

By visualizing the data stored in vector databases, users can gain a better understanding of complex relationships and make data-driven decisions more effectively.

Moreover, tools like Jupyter Notebook and Apache Zeppelin offer interactive coding environments that support various programming languages such as Python, R, and Scala.

These tools enable data scientists and analysts to write and execute code snippets in real-time, facilitating exploratory data analysis and model prototyping directly on the data stored in vector databases.

By leveraging these interactive coding environments, users can perform complex data transformations, apply machine learning algorithms, and visualize results seamlessly.

Furthermore, the integration of BI platforms like Looker or Mode Analytics with vector databases allows for interactive querying and data exploration without the need for deep technical expertise.

These platforms provide an intuitive drag-and-drop interface that simplifies the process of extracting insights from vector database data.

By enabling self-service analytics capabilities, organizations can empower business users across departments to access and analyze data autonomously, promoting a data-driven culture within the organization.

In conclusion, interactive analysis tools are essential for unlocking the full potential of vector databases by enabling real-time exploration and manipulation of data.

Visualization software, interactive coding environments, and BI platforms play a pivotal role in accelerating insights and improving decision-making processes.

By leveraging these tools in conjunction with vector databases, organizations can enhance their data analytics capabilities, drive innovation, and gain a competitive edge in today's data-driven landscape.

Chapter 32: Regulatory Compliance

Compliance Challenges in VDBs

Navigating regulatory compliance for vector databases

Compliance Challenges in VDBs

Regulatory compliance is a critical aspect for organizations dealing with vector databases due to the nature of the data they handle, especially when it comes to sensitive information.

One of the key challenges faced in this realm is ensuring adherence to data protection laws.

With the increasing focus on privacy and security, organizations must navigate a complex web of regulations such as GDPR, HIPAA, and CCPA, which impose strict requirements on how data is collected, stored, and processed.

Failing to meet these standards can result in severe penalties and reputational damage, making compliance a non-negotiable priority for businesses utilizing vector databases.

Another significant compliance challenge in vector databases revolves around industry-specific standards and regulations.

Different sectors, such as healthcare, finance, and government, have their own set of compliance requirements that organizations must comply with.

For instance, healthcare organizations dealing with patient data must adhere to HIPAA regulations, while financial institutions handling sensitive financial information are bound by regulations like PCI DSS. Navigating these industry standards alongside general data protection laws can be a complex endeavor, requiring a deep understanding of the specific requirements applicable to each sector.

To address the compliance challenges in vector databases effectively, organizations must develop comprehensive strategies that align with regulatory requirements while maximizing the utility of their databases.

This involves implementing robust security measures to safeguard data integrity and confidentiality, such as encryption, access controls, and data anonymization techniques.

Regular audits and compliance checks should also be conducted to ensure ongoing adherence to regulations and identify and rectify any potential non-compliance issues proactively.

Additionally, investing in staff training and awareness programs can help cultivate a culture of compliance within the organization, where employees understand their roles and responsibilities in upholding data protection standards.

In conclusion, navigating regulatory compliance in vector databases requires a proactive and holistic approach that encompasses both general data protection laws and industry-specific regulations.

By staying abreast of evolving compliance requirements, leveraging best practices in data security, and fostering a culture of compliance within the organization, businesses can mitigate the risks associated with non-compliance and build trust with their stakeholders.

Ultimately, compliance should not be viewed as a burdensome obligation but rather as a strategic imperative that enhances data governance and strengthens the overall cybersecurity posture of an organization.

Chapter 33: Regulatory Compliance

Auditing & Reporting Mechanisms

Implementing effective auditing and reporting in VDBs

To implement effective auditing and reporting in vector databases (VDBs), it is crucial to establish robust mechanisms to monitor and track all access and modifications to the data stored within the database.

Auditing and reporting play a vital role in maintaining regulatory compliance and ensuring data governance within organizations.

By focusing on the use of specialized tools and methodologies, businesses can streamline these processes to enhance transparency and accountability in their data management practices.

One fundamental aspect of auditing in VDBs involves setting up detailed access controls and logging mechanisms to track who accesses the database, when they access it, and what actions they perform.

This can be achieved by implementing authentication mechanisms, such as user accounts with specific permissions, to ensure that only authorized personnel have access to the data.

By recording all interactions with the database, organizations can create an audit trail that can be used to investigate any unauthorized activities or breaches.

Moreover, it is essential to monitor and audit modifications to the data stored in VDBs to ensure data integrity and reliability.

This can be done by employing techniques such as data versioning and checksums to track changes made to the database over time.

By maintaining a comprehensive record of alterations, organizations can easily identify any discrepancies or unauthorized modifications to the data.

Additionally, implementing encryption and data masking techniques can further secure sensitive information stored in the database, thus enhancing data protection measures.

In terms of reporting, organizations can leverage reporting tools and dashboards to generate insights and analytics based on the data stored in VDBs.

By creating customizable reports that align with regulatory requirements and internal policies, businesses can effectively communicate key metrics and findings to stakeholders.

Automated reporting processes can also help in saving time and reducing the margin of error in compliance reporting.

By combining auditing practices with robust reporting capabilities, organizations can not only demonstrate compliance but also drive informed decision-making processes based on data-driven insights extracted from their vector databases.

Chapter 34: Ethical Considerations

AI Ethics in Vector Databases

Ethical considerations in the use of vector databases in AI

AI Ethics in Vector Databases

Ethical considerations in the use of vector databases in AI are paramount as these technologies play a crucial role in shaping the future of data analytics.

One of the primary ethical concerns revolves around bias.

Bias in vector databases can lead to discriminatory outcomes in AI applications, perpetuating inequalities and reinforcing existing prejudices.

To address this, data scientists and AI engineers must be vigilant in identifying and mitigating biases present in the data used to train vector databases.

This includes conducting regular bias assessments, implementing fairness metrics, and utilizing techniques such as debiasing algorithms to ensure that AI systems built on vector databases are fair and unbiased.

Privacy is another ethical consideration that arises when using vector databases in AI. Vector databases store vast amounts of data, including sensitive information about individuals.

Protecting this data from unauthorized access, misuse, or data breaches is crucial to maintaining trust and safeguarding privacy rights.

Encryption techniques, strict data access controls, and anonymization methods can help mitigate privacy risks associated with vector databases.

Additionally, organizations must adhere to data privacy regulations such as GDPR and HIPAA to ensure that data is processed and stored ethically and legally.

Transparency is essential for fostering trust in AI systems built on vector databases.

Lack of transparency can lead to skepticism and suspicion among users and stakeholders, undermining the credibility of AI applications.

To address this concern, AI/ML Engineers or Architects must strive for transparency throughout the AI development lifecycle.

This includes documenting the data sources and processes involved in training vector databases, explaining the decision-making processes of AI algorithms, and providing clear insights into how AI systems make predictions or recommendations.

By promoting transparency, organizations can enhance accountability and empower users to understand and challenge the outputs of AI systems based on vector databases.

Chapter 35: Ethical Considerations

Bias in Vector Data

Addressing bias in vector data and databases

Title: Vector Databases Unleashed: Navigating the Future of Data Analytics

Section: Bias in Vector Data

Sub-Section Name: Addressing bias in vector data and databases

Sub-Section Brief: Understanding and mitigating bias in vector data is crucial for building fair and effective AI/ML systems.

This section examines the sources of bias in vector data, its impact on AI applications, and strategies for detecting and correcting bias within vector databases.

It provides a roadmap for ensuring data fairness and integrity.

In the realm of AI and machine learning, bias in vector data can introduce significant challenges, impacting the performance and reliability of algorithms.

One key aspect of addressing bias in vector data is to first identify its sources.

Bias can stem from multiple factors, including historical data collection practices, imbalanced datasets, human biases encoded in the data, and systemic inequalities reflected in the vectors.

By meticulously analyzing the data sources, data scientists and engineers can pinpoint where bias is originating from, enabling targeted mitigation strategies.

Once bias in vector data is identified, the next critical step is to mitigate its impact on AI applications.

This process involves implementing corrective measures within vector databases to address bias at its root.

Techniques such as data augmentation, feature engineering, and oversampling of underrepresented classes can help in diversifying the dataset and reducing bias.

Additionally, the integration of fairness-aware algorithms and regular bias audits can assist in continuously monitoring and adjusting for biases that may arise during the data lifecycle.

Collaborative efforts between domain experts, data scientists, and ethicists are essential in ensuring a comprehensive and inclusive approach to bias mitigation in vector databases.

To further enhance the integrity and fairness of AI/ML systems, continuous monitoring and evaluation of bias in vector data is imperative.

Leveraging advanced analytics tools and techniques, such as model explainability algorithms and fairness metrics, can provide deeper insights into the behavior of AI models and help in detecting subtle biases that may not be apparent at first glance.

By establishing robust protocols for bias detection and mitigation, organizations can uphold ethical standards, promote transparency, and build trust with users and stakeholders.

In the ever-evolving landscape of data analytics, staying vigilant against bias in vector data is not only a best practice but a moral imperative to ensure the responsible development and deployment of AI technologies.

Chapter 36: International Perspectives

Global Trends in VDB Adoption

Exploring the global adoption of vector databases

Global Trends in VDB Adoption

As the world moves towards an AI-driven future, the adoption of vector databases (VDBs) has been rapidly increasing on a global scale.

Organizations across various industries are recognizing the importance of efficient data storage and retrieval for powering their AI and ML applications.

Regional differences play a significant role in the adoption and implementation of VDBs.

In North America and Europe, where technological advancements are driving forces, the adoption rates are notably higher compared to other regions.

This can be attributed to the presence of a large number of tech companies and research institutions that are actively investing in AI and ML technologies.

On the other hand, regions like Asia and Africa are also catching up quickly, with a surge in VDB adoption seen in emerging economies where AI applications are being integrated into healthcare, finance, and e-commerce sectors.

Industry-specific use cases are another key factor influencing the global trends in VDB adoption.

In the healthcare sector, for instance, VDBs are being leveraged to store and analyze vast amounts of patient data for predictive analytics and personalized treatment plans.

Financial institutions are using VDBs to detect fraud, manage risk, and optimize trading strategies.

E-commerce companies are utilizing VDBs to enhance customer recommendations and personalize shopping experiences.

The versatility and scalability of VDBs make them a valuable asset across a wide range of industries.

In addition to industry-specific use cases, the growing popularity of IoT devices and the explosion of data generated by these devices are also driving the adoption of VDBs worldwide.

Despite the numerous benefits that VDBs offer, organizations face challenges in their adoption journey.

One of the primary challenges is the complexity of migrating existing systems to VDBs and integrating them with AI and ML applications.

The lack of skilled professionals who are proficient in managing VDBs and implementing ML algorithms is another hurdle that organizations need to overcome.

Data privacy and security concerns also pose a significant challenge, especially in regions with stringent data protection regulations.

To address these challenges, organizations need to invest in continuous training and upskilling of their workforce, partner with experts in the field, and implement robust data governance practices to ensure the security and privacy of their data.

By overcoming these challenges, organizations can harness the full potential of VDBs and drive innovation in their AI and ML initiatives on a global scale.

Chapter 37: International Perspectives

Cross-Border Data Management

Managing cross-border data flows with vector databases

Cross-Border Data Management with Vector Databases

In the realm of data analytics, managing cross-border data flows effectively and compliantly is a crucial consideration for organizations utilizing vector databases.

The intersection of international data transfers with the complexities of data analytics presents a unique challenge that requires a strategic approach.

To navigate this challenge successfully, organizations must address both the legal and technical aspects of cross-border data management.

From a legal perspective, compliance with data protection regulations such as the General Data Protection Regulation (GDPR) in Europe and the California Consumer Privacy Act (CCPA) in the United States is paramount when managing cross-border data flows.

Organizations must ensure that data sovereignty and privacy laws are upheld when transferring data across borders.

Vector databases, with their advanced data indexing and retrieval capabilities, can play a key role in ensuring that data is stored and accessed in compliance with relevant regulations.

Implementing encryption and anonymization techniques within vector databases can further strengthen data protection measures during cross-border transfers.

On the technical front, organizations leveraging vector databases for cross-border data management must focus on optimizing data transfer speeds and minimizing latency.

Leveraging cloud platforms and implementing efficient data replication strategies can help enhance the performance of cross-border data flows.

Additionally, organizations should prioritize data integrity and security by implementing robust authentication mechanisms and access controls within their vector database infrastructure.

By harnessing the scalability and flexibility of vector databases, organizations can achieve seamless cross-border data management while adhering to legal requirements and ensuring data security.

In conclusion, managing cross-border data flows with vector databases requires a holistic approach that encompasses legal compliance, technical optimization, and data security measures.

By integrating data protection best practices into their vector database infrastructure and leveraging advanced technologies for efficient data transfer, organizations can navigate the complexities of international data transfers effectively.

Continuous monitoring and adaptation to evolving regulatory landscapes are essential to ensure that cross-border data management remains compliant and secure in an increasingly globalized data environment.

Chapter 38: Career Development

Skills Development

Developing skills for careers in vector databases

Section: Building Expertise
Sub-Section Name: Skills Development
Sub-Section Brief: Developing skills for careers in vector databases

In the rapidly evolving landscape of data analytics, proficiency in vector databases is becoming increasingly critical for those aiming to excel in the field.

To embark on a successful career in vector databases, a diverse set of skills is required.

Firstly, a solid foundation in computer science or a related field, typically acquired through a degree or Ph.

D., forms the basis of expertise in this domain.

Understanding the principles of data structures, algorithms, and database management is fundamental.

Proficiency in programming languages such as Python, R, or Java is essential for implementing machine learning algorithms and deploying scalable solutions in vector databases.

Additionally, expertise in machine learning algorithms is indispensable for leveraging the full potential of vector databases.

Understanding how to apply algorithms efficiently, optimize performance, and interpret results is crucial.

Fluency in database management is another key skill as it involves designing, implementing, and optimizing database systems to ensure data integrity and efficiency.

Familiarity with various cloud platforms is beneficial, as many vector databases are deployed in cloud environments for scalability and flexibility.

Continuous learning and staying updated with the latest advancements in vector databases are essential to remain competitive in this dynamic field.

To develop these skills, aspiring professionals can pursue educational paths that provide specialized training in vector databases.

Enrolling in courses on machine learning, database management, and cloud computing can enhance one's knowledge and proficiency in these areas.

Obtaining relevant certifications, such as those in machine learning or cloud platforms, can also validate one's skills and expertise to potential employers.

Hands-on experience is invaluable for honing practical skills in deploying and managing vector databases.

Working on real-world projects or internships can provide the necessary exposure and expertise to excel in this field.

Moreover, staying engaged with industry trends, attending conferences, workshops, and networking events can broaden one's understanding of vector databases.

Collaborating with peers, participating in online communities, and sharing knowledge can further enhance skills and foster a culture of continuous learning.

Pursuing advanced certifications or specialized training programs can also deepen expertise in specific areas of vector databases, such as optimization algorithms or data visualization techniques.

By embracing a mindset of continuous improvement and being proactive in seeking out learning opportunities, professionals can shape a successful career in the dynamic and innovative field of vector databases.

Chapter 39: Career Development

Career Pathways in VDBs

Exploring career pathways in vector databases

Career Pathways in Vector Databases

As an expert in the field of vector databases, it's crucial to understand the diverse career pathways available within this dynamic ecosystem.

Starting with entry-level positions, individuals with a strong foundation in database management and data analytics can pursue roles such as Database Administrator or Data Analyst specializing in vector databases.

These roles involve maintaining database systems, ensuring data accuracy, and deriving insights from complex data structures.

For those looking to delve deeper into the technical aspects of vector databases, a career as an AI/ML Engineer or Architect could be an exciting path to explore.

This role requires expertise in machine learning algorithms, programming languages like Python or R, and experience with cloud platforms for deploying scalable solutions.

AI/ML engineers play a crucial role in optimizing vector database performance, developing innovative algorithms for data processing, and implementing advanced data analytics techniques.

As professionals gain more experience and expertise in the field of vector databases, they can progress towards specialized roles such as Vector Database Specialist or Solution Architect.

These roles involve working closely with clients to design customized database solutions, troubleshoot complex data issues, and optimize query performance for enhanced user experience.

Continuous learning and staying updated with the latest trends in vector databases are essential for professionals aspiring to excel in these advanced roles.

Furthermore, career pathways in vector databases also extend to leadership positions such as Chief Data Officer or Director of Data Science, where individuals are responsible for shaping the strategic direction of data initiatives within an organization.

These roles require a deep understanding of data governance, security protocols, and regulatory compliance, along with strong leadership skills to drive cross-functional teams towards achieving data-driven objectives.

By actively seeking out opportunities for professional development, certifications, and networking within the vector database community, professionals can chart a successful and rewarding career path in this cutting-edge field.

In conclusion, the field of vector databases offers a wealth of career opportunities for individuals with a passion for data analytics and a knack for problem-solving.

Whether starting out as a Database Administrator or aiming for a leadership position as a Chief Data Officer, professionals in this field have a wide range of career pathways to explore.

By honing their technical skills, staying abreast of industry trends, and actively seeking out mentorship and learning opportunities, individuals can navigate their way towards a fulfilling and impactful career in the fast-evolving world of vector databases.

Chapter 40: Future Outlook

Next-Generation VDB Tech

Anticipating future technologies in vector databases

In the realm of vector databases, future technological advancements hold immense potential to revolutionize data analytics and machine learning capabilities.

As we look ahead to the next generation of vector database technology, several key areas are likely to see significant developments.

One area of anticipated innovation is in hardware advancements tailored specifically for handling vector data efficiently.

Hardware acceleration has the potential to significantly enhance the performance of vector database operations, enabling faster query processing and more complex analyses.

We can expect to see specialized hardware solutions that are optimized for vector operations, such as custom processors or accelerators designed to streamline the computational tasks inherent in processing high-dimensional data.

Furthermore, ongoing research in algorithm development is poised to bring forth a new wave of sophisticated techniques for managing and querying vector data.

Advanced algorithms tailored for vector databases could offer improvements in indexing, similarity search, and dimensionality reduction, among other key tasks.

These algorithmic enhancements have the potential to boost the scalability and efficiency of vector databases, enabling them to handle increasingly large and complex datasets with greater speed and accuracy.

On the application front, the integration of vector databases with emerging technologies like edge computing, IoT, and real-time data analytics is expected to open up new opportunities for leveraging vector data in diverse use cases.

By bridging the gap between vector databases and cutting-edge technologies, organizations can harness the power of high-dimensional data in novel ways, ranging from personalized recommendations in e-commerce to predictive maintenance in industrial IoT systems.

This convergence of vector databases with other innovative technologies is likely to drive the development of new applications and solutions that capitalize on the unique strengths of vector data structures.

In conclusion, the future of vector databases holds immense promise, with anticipated advancements in hardware, algorithms, and applications that are set to redefine the landscape of data analytics and machine learning.

By embracing these cutting-edge technologies and innovations, organizations can unlock new possibilities for managing, analyzing, and deriving insights from high-dimensional data, ultimately paving the way for a new era of data-driven decision-making and AI innovation.

As we navigate the evolving landscape of vector database technology, continuous exploration and adaptation to these future advancements will be key to staying at the forefront of the field.

Chapter 41: Future Outlook

Societal Impact of VDBs

Assessing the societal impact of vector databases

Societal Impact of Vector Databases

Vector databases have emerged as a transformative technology with the potential to revolutionize various aspects of society.

One key area where vector databases can make a substantial impact is in healthcare.

By leveraging the power of vector representations, healthcare professionals can more effectively analyze patient data to make accurate diagnoses, personalize treatment plans, and ultimately improve patient outcomes.

For example, with the ability to efficiently process vast amounts of medical data, vector databases can assist in identifying patterns and correlations that may not be immediately evident through traditional methods.

This can lead to earlier detection of diseases, optimized treatment strategies, and overall better healthcare delivery.

Moreover, the use of vector databases in personalized digital experiences has the potential to reshape how consumers interact with technology and services.

By capturing and analyzing user preferences, behavior patterns, and feedback in real-time, companies can provide highly tailored and engaging experiences to their customers.

From personalized product recommendations to targeted advertising, vector databases play a vital role in enhancing user satisfaction and loyalty.

However, it is critical to navigate this aspect ethically to ensure that user privacy is respected, and data usage is transparent and secure.

Despite the numerous benefits that vector databases offer, there are also significant societal challenges that need to be addressed to mitigate potential risks.

One of the primary concerns revolves around data privacy and security.

As vector databases accumulate vast amounts of sensitive information, there is a pressing need to establish robust data governance frameworks and implement stringent security measures to safeguard against breaches and unauthorized access.

Additionally, the potential for biases in data-driven decision-making poses ethical dilemmas that must be carefully managed.

It is imperative for organizations utilizing vector databases to proactively address issues related to algorithmic bias, fairness, and accountability to ensure equitable outcomes for all individuals.

In conclusion, the societal impact of vector databases is multifaceted, offering tremendous opportunities for innovation and progress across various sectors.

However, to harness the full potential of this technology responsibly, it is essential for stakeholders to actively engage with the ethical and societal implications of their work.

By promoting transparency, accountability, and inclusivity in the development and deployment of vecto databases, we can amplify the positive benefits while mitigating potential risks.

Ultimately, a thoughtful and holistic approach to leveraging vector databases can lead to a more ethical equitable, and sustainable future for data analytics and societal progress as a whole.

Exploring Uncharted Realms: A Consciousness-Driven Narrative

- "This book takes a fresh and unconventional approach, prioritizing the depth of its content over traditional formatting."

- "In the spirit of embracing new perspectives, this book goes beyond traditional conventions to delve into the core of its content, offering valuable insights and raising awareness."

- "I invite you to explore this book as a departure from the traditional, as its focus lies in delivering meaningful content that inspires awareness and personal growth."

- "Rather than adhering to traditional book structures, this work is a conscious effort to prioritize the substance of its content, providing readers with thought-provoking insights and fostering a deeper understanding."

- "With an emphasis on content-driven exploration, this book aims to challenge conventional norms and stimulate awareness, offering readers a unique and thought-provoking reading experience."

- "Through its unconventional approach, this book seeks to engage readers in a meaningful dialogue, encouraging them to think critically and explore new perspectives beyond the confines of traditional formats."

- "As you embark on this unconventional reading journey, I encourage you to embrace the uncharted territory, where content and awareness take center stage, transcending the boundaries of traditional book structures."